Building
Bookcases

PATRICK PEDAVOLI

GREG CHEETHAM

MINI · WORKBOOK · SERIES

MEREHURST

CONTENTS

*Simple shelves with brackets (opposite above),
modular units with optional doors (opposite below
left), bookcase with pull-out desk (left)*

Planning your bookcase

Bookcases do not have to be plain and uninspiring in order to be functional. They can be attractive pieces of furniture in their own right, as well as practical, versatile storage and display units.

PLANNING

When planning extra shelving to hold your book collection, take into account the number of books, their sizes, and whether there is a need for easy access and/or protective storage. If space is at a premium, remember that you may be able to construct built-in shelves that wrap around doors or windows.

WEIGHT LOAD

A major consideration in building a bookcase is the weight that the shelf or shelves will have to support— which, in the case of even a small collection of paperbacks, is quite substantial. The weight load will affect your choice of materials, construction methods, the thickness of shelves, the width of shelf spans and the types of joints or brackets you will use to support the shelves. Bookcases are often built using housed joints, as these support more weight than other kinds of joints.

For wider bookcases the spacing between the supports is important, and depends on the weight load as well as the type of timber or board used. Thicker timbers will bear more books compared with lightweight boards. For units made of lightweight materials such as chipboard or thin MDF (medium density fibreboard), a plywood or hardwood back will provide extra strength.

Wall-mounted bookshelves will be under particular stress and must be fixed securely. The fixing method depends on whether your home is of solid masonry or frame construction, and on the weight load.

POSITIONING SHELVES

You can use adjustable or fixed shelving, or both. If you have large 'coffee table' books, or you want to display ornaments as well as books, adjustable shelving would allow you to adjust shelf heights to suit.

Fixed shelves are usually stronger than adjustable shelves. Position some fixed shelves far enough apart to accommodate your tallest books, allowing a few centimetres clearance above the height of the books so they are easy to remove and return.

Shelves should be deep enough to stop books from sitting right on (or over) the edge, but not so deep that books are pushed to the back of the unit making them difficult to retrieve.

Taller, deeper shelves should be positioned towards the bottom of the bookcase, to provide stability and

Plan your bookcase design carefully. This will help you to maximize available storage and ensure that shelves are sufficiently sturdy for your purposes.

easy access to the back of the shelves. It is much easier to lift heavier or more frequently used books from the lower and centre shelves than from the shelves at the top of the unit, which could be reserved for rarely handled or valuable items.

CARING FOR YOUR BOOKS

Books should be stored upright rather than on their sides, which can scuff the covers. If you have a valuable collection, place the shelves for those books away from direct sunlight and fluorescent lighting.

Make sure you don't pack your books too tightly together. To avoid too much wear and tear on a book, remove it by grasping it on either side of the spine, rather than using a finger to tease it out of the shelf by the top of the spine.

Although these shelves are designed to hold books, they could also be adapted for use as kitchen storage or general display shelving. Ash timber was used to build the shelves shown here.

Simple shelves with brackets

These easy-to-make timber shelves are supported by brackets that can be left as solid timber pieces or decorated with diamond-shaped cut-outs. Moulded edges provide a professional finish.

TOOLS

- Tape measure and pencil
- Combination square
- Pair of safety glasses
- Dust mask
- Hearing protection
- Panel saw or circular saw
- Electric jigsaw or coping saw

- Tenon saw
- Smoothing plane or jack plane
- Rebate plane
- Electric router
- Router bit: 45 degree bevel cutter
- Chisel: 25 mm
- Six G-cramps

- Electric drill
- Drill bits: 3 mm, 4 mm, 5 mm, 8 mm, 10 mm countersink
- Utility knife
- Cork sanding block
- Flat file
- Screwdriver: cross-head
- Spirit level

CUTTING THE PARTS

1 Lay the timber on a workbench, and mark out the parts with a tape measure and square. Check that the pieces are square and straight.

2 Wearing safety glasses, cut out the parts using a panel saw or a circular saw, then lightly plane the pieces. Label the pieces on the inside face for easy identification, and mark the face side and edge. Use a square to check for accuracy on all edges and faces.

SHAPING AND JOINING SHELVES AND FIXING RAILS

3 After you have cut them to length, check the two shelves and two fixing rails to make sure that the face edges are square and parallel.

4 Mark along each shelf with a marking gauge set to the thickness of the fixing rail (19 mm), then cut a rebate 13 mm deep using a rebate plane or a router. If you are using a router, attach a fence and an 18 mm straight cutter. Move along the back edge of the shelf piece, taking out 5 mm at a time (see the box on page 11 for information about using a router). Leave at least 6 mm at the top of the rebate.

5 Take the 2100 mm back fixing rail and mark the centre. On the back of the rail, mark 50 mm in from either end of the rail. Starting and finishing at the marked 50 mm positions, measure and mark eight 250 mm wide spacings. Using a marking

MATERIALS★

Part	Material	Finished length	No.
Shelf	250 x 25 mm timber PAR	2100 mm	2
Back fixing rail	100 x 25 mm timber PAR	2100 mm	2
Bracket	250 x 25 mm timber PAR	300 mm	6

OTHER: Thirty 50 mm x no. 6 cross-head countersunk screws; wall fixings (see step 17); PVA adhesive; cloths; abrasive paper: four sheets of 180 grit and three sheets of 240 grit; clear lacquer or finish of your choice

★For two shelves. Finished size: 319 mm high (base of bracket to top of shelf); 2100 mm long; 238 mm deep. For timber sizes and styles see page 64. Timber sizes given are nominal.

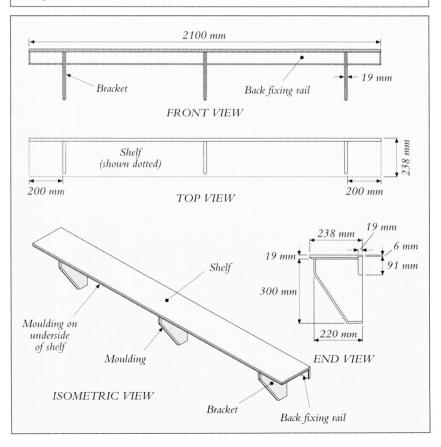

FRONT VIEW

TOP VIEW

END VIEW

ISOMETRIC VIEW

gauge, measure and mark 7 mm down from the top edge to the lines you have just drawn. Where the lines cross, drill a 4 mm hole right through. Countersink all the holes.

6 Put the two shelves on your workbench and cut the moulded edges with a router, using a bevel cutter shape. Mould the underside of each shelf on the two short end edges first, then on the long front edge.

7 Set the fixing rail in the rebate on the shelf, face side out. Mark the depth of the rebate onto the rail. Cut mouldings on the ends of the rail, up to the pencil marks, and on the bottom edge of the rail.

8 Sand all the moulded edges to a smooth finish with 180 grit abrasive paper. Join the back fixing rail to the shelf to check the fit, apply adhesive to the rebate and cramp the fixing rail to the shelf with G-cramps. Drill 3 mm pilot holes, then screw the fixing rail to the shelf. Wipe off excess adhesive with a damp cloth and leave to dry.

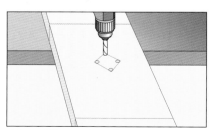

11 Drill on the inside of the four points of the diamond and cut out the rest of the shape with a jigsaw.

MAKING THE BRACKETS

9 Cut the six bracket pieces to 300 mm long and 220 mm wide, and mark out a top and a face edge.

10 Make the cut-out before marking out the basic bracket (see the diagram on page 10). Working from the top 220 mm side, measure straight down 130 mm and draw a horizontal line parallel to the top. Then, from the back 300 mm side, measure straight across 100 mm and draw a vertical line parallel to the side. Measuring from the centre, where the lines cross come up and mark 30 mm, then mark down 30 mm, across 30 mm and back 30 mm to form a diamond.

11 Use an 8 mm drill bit to drill on the inside of the four points of the diamond, and then cut out the rest of the shape with a jigsaw or a coping saw. Clean up the edges of the cut-out with a file, then mould the edges of the diamond.

12 Now mark the basic bracket shape (see the diagram on page 10). Starting at the top of a 300 mm side, measure 70 mm straight down along the edge and mark the position. Working from what will be the bottom edge of the bracket, measure 70 mm straight across along the edge and mark. With a combination square and pencil, draw a straight line joining the two marks. Trace over the lines with a utility knife and cut out the shape with a panel saw or circular saw.

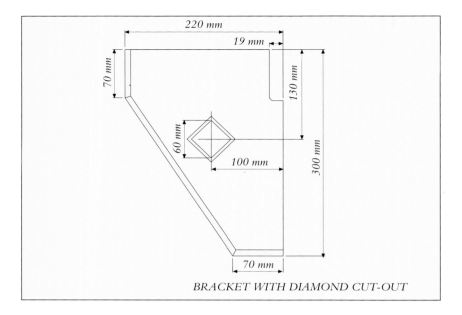

220 mm

19 mm

70 mm

130 mm

60 mm

100 mm

300 mm

70 mm

BRACKET WITH DIAMOND CUT-OUT

13 Mark out the back of the bracket for a cut-out to accommodate the moulded edge of the fixing rail. Place each shelf on the bench and sit the bracket on the shelf. Position the bracket against the rail, then use a square to mark a straight line across the back edge of the bracket at 90 degrees. Place the bracket back on the bench. Set up the marking gauge

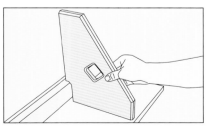

13 Cut out the excess from the back edge of the bracket and check the fit against the fixing rail.

at 19 mm, and mark downwards to indicate the area to be cut out. Cut out the excess from the back edge of the bracket and check the fit against the fixing rail. Sand with 180 grit abrasive paper.

14 Rout a moulding along the three outside edges of the bracket, not cutting too deeply. Don't shape the edge that fits to the wall and the shelf.

ASSEMBLING THE BRACKETS AND SHELVES

15 Lay each shelf down on the workbench with the fixing rail facing up, and mark the positions where you will attach the brackets. Find the centre of the rail and mark a vertical line with your square, then measure 210 mm in from either end and again

The edges of the cut-outs are decorated with mouldings.

mark vertical lines. Measure 20 mm and 60 mm down these lines and mark horizontal lines across, to find the centre position for the screw holes. Where the lines cross, drill 4 mm holes, then countersink.

16 Sand all parts with 180 grit abrasive paper, then with 220 grit. Apply adhesive to the top and back edges of the brackets and the shelves where the brackets will be attached. Clamp the pieces together. Remove excess adhesive with a damp cloth. Fasten the shelves and brackets with 50 mm x no. 6 countersunk crosshead screws.

INSTALLING THE SHELVES

17 How you fit the walls to the shelves will depend on the wall construction. For masonry walls, use at least four 50 mm x no. 10 countersunk screws with wall plugs

USING A ROUTER

- Use cramps or a vice to secure the work.
- Always do a test cut on a scrap piece to check the router settings.
- Wear safety glasses, hearing protection and a dust mask.
- When cutting straight grooves and slots, use the supplied guide fence, or clamp a straight piece of timber to the work and run the base plate of the router firmly along it. Set the router to depth and run it back and forth along the piece to remove all waste.
- Don't cut to the required size the first time. Always make two or three passes with the router.
- If the router sticks, wipe along the fence with soap or candlewax.
- If your router skips and leaves a dent, fill the dent with a plastic filler that sets hard, or an epoxy version, and run the groove again.

of the appropriate size. Nylon anchors are an alternative. If very heavy objects will be placed on the shelves, use 75 x 6.5 mm expansion bolts. For timber-framed walls, you will need to locate the studs behind the lining to determine the spacings; you should use 50 mm x no. 10 countersunk screws at the least. Fix one fastening first, then bring the shelf to the level position, checking with a spirit level. Drill the wall and fix the second fastening. Test that each shelf is level and adjust before securing with the final fastenings.

Child's bookcase

This whimsical 'boatshed' style MDF bookcase, with decorative trim on the shelves and roof, is perfect for a child's room. It lends itself to a brightly coloured paint scheme.

TOOLS

- Tape measure or rule
- Combination square
- Builders square
- Pencil
- Pair of safety glasses
- Dust mask
- Hearing protection
- Smoothing plane or jack plane
- Jigsaw or coping saw
- Tenon saw
- Panel saw or circular saw
- Four G-cramps
- Hammer
- Electric drill
- Drill bits: 3 mm, 5 mm, 10 mm countersink
- Electric router
- Router bit: 12 mm twin-flute flush cutter
- File
- Cork sanding block
- Screwdriver (cross-head)
- Filler knife
- Compass (optional)

CUTTING OUT

1 Lay the MDF on a bench and mark out the parts with a tape measure and combination square.

2 Wearing safety glasses and a dust mask, cut out the parts with a panel saw or circular saw. Use a smoothing plane or jack plane to smooth the edges and bring all parts to their finished size, checking that you are planing square. Label all pieces on the inside face to identify them. A timber merchant may be able to cut the MDF to size for you.

MAKING FRONT APRONS

3 Pencil a half-pattern for the front shelf aprons in freehand on the 400 mm long plywood (or use a ruler and compass). Only draw a half-pattern—it will be traced on to one half of the apron, then repeated in mirror image on the other half. Cut out the template with a jigsaw or coping saw. Clean it up with a file.

4 Take one of the 764 x 54 mm front aprons and mark a centre line

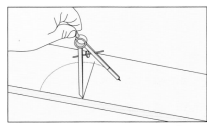

4 Using a compass, come up 2 mm from the bottom edge and mark a 54 mm diameter semicircle.

The decorative patterns on the shelf and roof aprons were marked on the MDF by re-usable plywood templates. The designs for the patterns can be drawn freehand or marked out using a ruler and a compass.

MATERIALS★

Part	Material	Length	Width	No.
End panel	18 mm MDF	1200 mm	400 mm	2
Top panel	18 mm MDF	764 mm	400 mm	1
Shelf	18 mm MDF	764 mm	400 mm	4
Front apron for upper, centre and lower shelves	18 mm MDF	764 mm	54 mm	3
Front apron for bottom shelf★★	18 mm MDF	764 mm	80 mm	2
Roof apron	18 mm MDF	563 mm	70 mm	2
Roof panel	18 mm MDF	600 mm	400 mm	2
Back☆	4 mm MDF	1550 mm	796 mm	1
Template for front aprons	3 mm plywood	400 mm	54 mm	1
Template for roof aprons	3 mm plywood	600 mm	70 mm	1

OTHER: Sixty 25 mm flat-head nails; twenty 10 mm brad nails; eight 28 mm x no. 8 countersunk screws; twenty 32 mm x no. 8 countersunk screws; thirty-two 40 mm x no. 8 countersunk screws; PVA adhesive; cloths; abrasive paper: two sheets of 120 grit and four sheets of 180 grit; plastic wood filler; paint of your choice

★Finished size: 1625 mm high; 850 mm wide; 400 mm deep.
★★One for front (to be shaped), one for back (not shaped).
☆To be cut at assembly stage.

with a combination square. Using a compass at the centre line, come up 2 mm from the bottom edge and mark a 54 mm diameter semicircle.

5 Place the template on the front apron piece, aligning it with the centre line. Trace the shape, then flip the template over and trace the shape on the other side of the centre line. Remove the template. Fix the apron on to the bench with G-cramps and

cut out the rough shape with a jigsaw or coping saw, cutting on the waste side of the line and leaving 3–5 mm excess. Fasten the template back on to the apron with 10 mm brad nails.

6 Clamp the apron and attached template to the bench. Using a jigsaw or coping saw, or a router with a 12 mm flush cutter, cut around the template (see page 11 for information on routers). Remove the

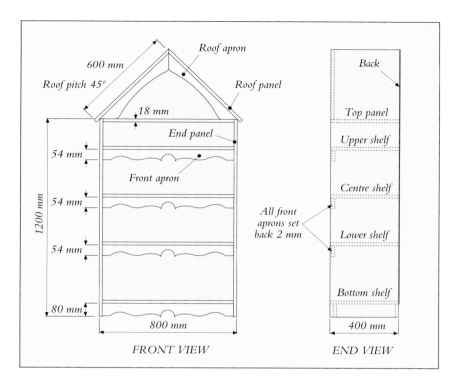

Roof apron

600 mm

Roof pitch 45°

Roof panel

18 mm

End panel

54 mm

Front apron

54 mm

All front
aprons set
back 2 mm

54 mm

1200 mm

80 mm

800 mm

FRONT VIEW

Back

Top panel

Upper shelf

Centre shelf

Lower shelf

Bottom shelf

400 mm

END VIEW

template. File the curved profile to remove rough edges and sand with 120 grit abrasive paper. This piece is the template for the remaining front aprons, including the 80 mm wide bottom apron. Repeat the cutting-out process for all front aprons.

ASSEMBLING THE SHELVES

7 Take the shelves and measure and mark 50 mm in from either end and 10 mm in from the front edge. Drill and countersink 5 mm holes. Mark three equally spaced screw positions between the 50 mm marks (see the diagram on page 16), and drill and countersink 5 mm holes.

8 Apply adhesive to the top edge of one front apron and clamp it to the shelf, ensuring the ends are flush and the front of the apron is set back 2 mm. Drill 3 mm pilot holes and use 32 mm x no. 8 countersunk screws to secure the apron. Remove excess adhesive with a damp cloth and repeat the process for all aprons.

9 Take the end panels and mark out the position of the top panel and the shelves on inside and outside faces. Lay the shelves on the bench at right angles to one end panel. Drill 5 mm holes in the end panels, and then countersink so that the screw heads

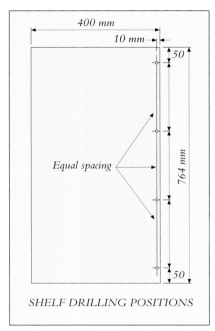

400 mm

10 mm

50

Equal spacing

764 mm

50

SHELF DRILLING POSITIONS

11 Take one roof piece and on the mitred edge mark a screw position 50 mm in from each end and 10 mm back from the mitred edge. Mark another screw position halfway between the two 50 mm marks. Drill 5 mm clearance holes and then countersink 10 mm. On the other mitred edge of the roof, mark a screw position 125 mm in from each end and 10 mm back from the facing edge. Drill 5 mm screw holes and countersink as before.

12 Place the roof pieces together to drill 3 mm pilot holes. Glue the mitred ends, hold them together, and fasten with 40 mm x no. 8 counter-sunk screws.

MAKING THE ROOF APRONS

13 Draw an arched shape as a pattern for the roof aprons (this time draw a complete pattern). For the front aprons, make a template for the roof aprons and cut and rout to shape.

14 Place the aprons on the bench. Use a square to mark a 45-degree

finish 1–2 mm below the surface. Spread adhesive where the top panel and shelves will join the end panel, and fasten the pieces with 40 mm x no. 8 countersunk screws. Repeat for the other end panel. Remove excess adhesive. Fill screw holes with plastic filler, leave to dry, and sand with 120 grit abrasive paper.

MITRING THE ROOF PIECES

10 Place the two roof pieces on the bench and mitre the top joining ends. Use a combination square to mark each 45 degree mitre, then square a line across each side. Cut the angle with a circular saw or panel saw, or simply plane the mitre, then check the fit and if necessary adjust by planing.

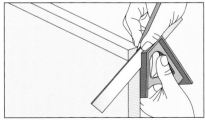

10 Use a combination square to mark each 45-degree mitre, then square a line across each side.

Mitred joints are used to fasten the basic roof panels as well as the shaped roof aprons.

angle on the ends to be joined, and cut out the mitres.

15 Lay the roof on its back edge, with the facing edge up towards you. For each side, mark three screw positions 10 mm in from the facing edge, the first 100 mm in from the top mitred end, the other two at intervals of 220 mm. Drill 5 mm holes and countersink as before.

16 Glue and clamp the apron pieces to the roof assembly, flush with the front. Drill 3 mm pilot holes into the aprons and use 32 mm x no. 8 countersunk screws to secure the aprons. Ensure that the screw heads are below the surface before filling them with filler. Leave to dry, then sand with 120 grit abrasive paper.

ASSEMBLING THE UNIT
17 Align the roof assembly on the base unit. Measure and mark out three screw positions on each roof panel, then drill 5 mm clearance holes at these positions through the roof panels. Countersink the screw holes in preparation for filling them. Use a 3 mm bit to make pilot holes for the screws.

18 Using 28 mm x no. 8 countersunk screws, fasten the assembled roof to the base unit. Fill the screw holes with plastic filler, and leave to dry. When the filler has dried completely, sand it flush with 120 grit abrasive paper.

19 Lay the unit face down. Place the back piece into position to check the fit, then pencil in a cutting line. Using a panel saw, cut the back to size, planing off any rough edges. Fasten with 25 mm flat-head nails.

20 Sand the entire unit with 180 grit abrasive paper. Undercoat it and paint in the colour of your choice.

The tapered design of these easily assembled units provides a deep storage area for larger items in the lower shelves. Aprons attached to the shelves ensure that your books remain neatly in place when you wheel the bookcases around.

Hinged bookcases on casters

This versatile piece comprises two units hinged together. The units are mounted on casters and can be positioned back to back to save space, or side by side to serve as a room divider.

MATERIALS*

PART	MATERIAL	LENGTH	WIDTH	NO.
End panel	18 mm MDF	1400 mm	450 mm	4
Bottom shelf	18 mm MDF	914 mm	418 mm	2
Lower shelf	18 mm MDF	914 mm	342 mm	2
Centre shelf	18 mm MDF	914 mm	267 mm	2
Upper shelf	18 mm MDF	914 mm	206 mm	2
Top panel	18 mm MDF	914 mm	187 mm	2
Kicker	18 mm MDF	914 mm	153 mm	2
Front apron	18 mm MDF	914 mm	60 mm	6
Back	12 mm MDF	914 mm	1400 mm	2
Cleat (side)	19 x 19 mm timber PAR	375 mm		4
Cleat (front/back)	19 x 19 mm timber PAR	912 mm		4

OTHER: 160 of 40 mm x no. 6 countersunk cross-head screws; forty 32 mm x no. 6 countersunk cross-head screws; one 1400 mm piano hinge or four 50 mm butt hinges; PVA adhesive; cloths; eight 100 mm high casters; plastic wood filler; 35 x 6 mm panhead bolts, nuts and washers for casters; abrasive paper: two sheets of 120 grit and six sheets of 180 grit; paint of your choice

*Finished size (single unit): 1400 mm high; 950 mm wide; 450 mm deep.

CUTTING OUT

1 Lay the pieces of MDF on a bench, and mark out the parts with a tape measure and square.

2 Wearing safety glasses and a dust mask, cut out the parts using a panel saw or a circular saw and guide. Cut all parts slightly oversize, and smooth back the rough edges to the correct size with a smoothing plane or jack plane. Alternatively, a timber merchant or cabinetmaker may be able to cut the MDF for you.

TOOLS

- Tape measure
- Steel rule: 300 mm
- Combination square
- Pencil
- Pair of safety glasses
- Dust mask
- Vice

- Smoothing plane or jack plane
- Electric drill
- Drill bits: 3 mm, 5 mm, 6 mm, 10 mm countersink
- Screwdriver (cross-head)

- Panel saw or portable circular saw
- Filler knife
- Orbital sander (optional)
- Cork sanding block
- Hammer

3 For the sloping sides of the end panels, measure and mark a point 200 mm along what will be the narrow top edge of each end panel. Measure and mark 153 mm up from the base of the long side. Use the steel rule to draw a straight line joining the two marks. Cut along the line, then smooth back with a plane.

PREPARING THE APRONS AND KICKER

4 Take the front aprons and mark screw positions, starting 50 mm in from each end and 10 mm up from the bottom edge. Mark three equally spaced screw positions between the first two 50 mm marks. Drill 5 mm screw holes and countersink so

the screw heads will finish 1–2 mm below the surface, ready for filling. Mark and drill corresponding 3 mm pilot holes in the front edges of the shelves. Place each shelf in a vice.

5 Glue and screw the joining edges of the aprons and shelves, removing excess adhesive with a damp cloth. Secure aprons with 40 mm x no. 6 countersunk cross-head screws.

6 Place the kicker on the bench. Measuring from the bottom edge, use a steel rule to mark one line across at 104 mm. Drill holes along this line as you did for the front apron. Carefully drill 5 mm holes and countersink as in step 4. Mark a line

5 Glue and screw the joining edges. Secure aprons with 40 mm x no. 6 countersunk cross-head screws.

7 Mark out the centre lines of the shelf positions from the bottom edge of each end panel.

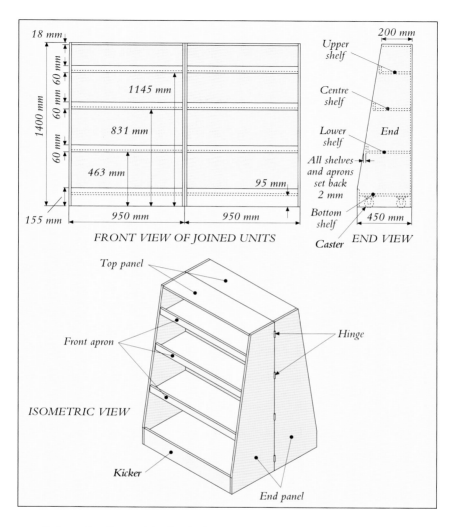

FRONT VIEW OF JOINED UNITS

END VIEW

ISOMETRIC VIEW

parallel to the line with the holes 95 mm from the base of the kicker. Align the shelf to the line, checking as you go. Drill 3 mm pilot holes in the front edge of the bottom shelf and then fasten the kicker using 40 mm x no. 6 countersunk cross-head screws.

ATTACHING THE SHELVES AND APRONS

7 Lay the two pairs of side panels on the bench, back edge to back edge. Mark out the centre lines of the shelf positions from the bottom edge of each end panel. The first line will be 104 mm up, the next 472 mm, then

When opened out, these hinged units serve as a multipurpose room divider. The shelves and attached aprons are set back from the front edge of the end panels.

840 mm and 1154 mm respectively. Mark a line 9 mm down from the narrow top edge.

8 Measure in along each line 50 mm from the front and back edges. The top and the two shelves below each

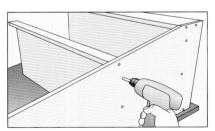

9 Ensure that the shelf is square to the end panel and then insert the remaining screws.

need only two screws at either end. The bottom three shelves require three screws, evenly spaced. Drill 5 mm clearance holes at each of these points and countersink as for step 4.

9 Take one end panel and the bottom shelf. Align them accurately before inserting the top 40 mm x no. 8 countersunk screw. Ensure that the shelf is square to the end panel, and insert the remaining two screws. Repeat for all shelves. The top panel must be flush with the top of the end panels and is set back 2 mm.

10 Turn the unit on its end. Apply adhesive to the ends of the shelves.

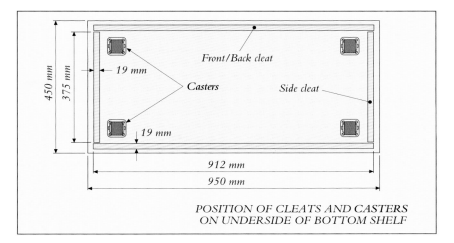

450 mm
375 mm
19 mm
Front/Back cleat
Casters
Side cleat
19 mm
912 mm
950 mm

*POSITION OF CLEATS AND CASTERS
ON UNDERSIDE OF BOTTOM SHELF*

Align the end panel on the shelves and fasten each shelf with screws. Remove excess adhesive. Insert two screws through each end into the kicker, then countersink.

11 Check that the backs have been cut to the correct size and are square. Lay the units face down and apply a bead of adhesive to the perimeter of each unit, then position the back. Use four 40 mm x no. 6 countersunk screws down each side and three screws in each shelf to secure the back. Ensure the end panels and top are flush with the back edges. Countersink the screws.

ATTACHING THE CLEATS AND CASTERS
12 Secure cleats to the underside of the unit: fix the two 912 mm cleats to the front and back edges with ten screws each, and the two 375 mm cleats to the side edges with six screws. Drill evenly spaced, 5 mm screw holes and countersink. Glue the joining surfaces, drill 3 mm pilot holes and attach cleats with 32 mm x no. 6 countersunk screws. Wipe off excess adhesive.

13 Mark positions for casters in each corner of the underside of the unit, close to the edge. Hold each caster in place, drill 6 mm holes and attach with 35 mm x 6 mm panhead bolts.

FINISHING THE UNITS
14 Use a filler knife to fill screw holes with plastic wood filler. Leave to dry, then sand with 120 grit abrasive paper. Paint as you prefer.

15 On the back joining edge of each unit, mark 50 mm down from the top, 50 mm up from the bottom and two positions in between. Position each hinge, bore pilot holes, then drive in screws to fasten.

Diamond-shaped bookshelves

Timbers of contrasting colours are used for this piece of fine furniture. Skill in using a router is essential for making the dovetail splines that fasten the shelves and supports.

TOOLS

- Rule: 300 mm and 1 m
- Tape measure
- Pencil
- Combination square
- Marking gauge
- Pair of safety glasses
- Dust mask
- Hearing protection
- Smoothing plane or jack plane

- Panel saw (optional)
- Portable circular saw
- Tenon saw
- Vice or suitable workbench
- Electric router
- Router bit: 15 mm dovetail
- Sliding bevel
- Protractor
- Electric drill

- Drill bit: 5 mm, 10 mm countersink
- Four G-cramps
- Six 600 mm sash cramps
- Round paintbrush: 12 mm
- Hammer
- Screwdriver
- Cork sanding block
- Utility knife

PREPARATION

1 Timber must be straight, square and defect-free. Season the timber by stacking it for a month in the room where the shelves will be installed. This reduces the chance of shrinkage.

2 For this project, have your timber merchant supply the timber at the finished sizes given in the Materials list. Draw a full-sized set-out on 4 mm MDF, setting the dovetail joints out on a centre line. The set-out should correspond to the thicknesses of your purchased timber.

3 You must also make a jig for cutting dovetail joints and splines.

CUTTING OUT

4 Using a jack plane or smoothing plane, dress the diagonal supports and shelves to their finished width of 225 mm.

5 With a combination square and tape measure, mark the lengths of the shelves and diagonal supports. Leave 5–10 mm space between the pieces for saw cuts. Check the dimensions against the set-out, then continue the lines over the edges and across the back face of the timber.

6 Score the lines with a utility knife. Cut the pieces to length and smooth the ends with a smoothing plane.

All components were laid out on an MDF set-out at final assembly to help in piecing together the correct diamond shape. The shelves and fixing rails are made of silver ash, the supports and dovetail splines of cedar.

MATERIALS★

Part	Material	Length	No.
Centre shelf	225 x 24 mm light timber	1200 mm	1
Upper and lower shelf	225 x 24 mm light timber	800 mm	2
Top shelf and base	225 x 24 mm light timber	400 mm	2
Fixing rail★★	31 x 19 mm light timber	3000 mm	1
Diagonal support	225 x 24 mm dark timber	278 mm	8
End lipping★★	41 x 24 mm dark timber	4200 mm	1
Dovetail spline★★	19 x 12 mm dark timber	4200 mm	2
Base for set-out	4 mm MDF	1200 x 1200 mm	1

OTHER: Ten 40 mm x no. 8 cross-head screws; wall fixings (see steps 24 and 25); PVA adhesive; cloths; abrasive paper: six sheets of 180 grit and four sheets of 220 grit; clear lacquer or finish of your choice
For the jig table: One piece of 12 mm MDF 350 mm long x 180 mm wide.
For the jig fence: One piece of 18 mm MDF 350 mm long x 50 mm wide.

★Finished size: 1200 mm high; 1200 mm wide; 225 mm deep. Finished timber sizes are given here. For timber types and timber sizes, see the box on page 64.
★★To be cut later into the required number of pieces.

MACHINING THE DOVETAIL HOUSINGS ON A JIG TABLE

7 Make a central hole in the 12 mm MDF for the dovetail cutter. Remove the router base and replace it with the MDF. Set the router in a suitable workbench or vice.

8 Clamp an 18 mm MDF fence to the router base. Set the router to cut

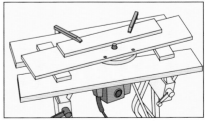

7 Remove the router base and replace it with the MDF. Set the router in a suitable workbench or vice.

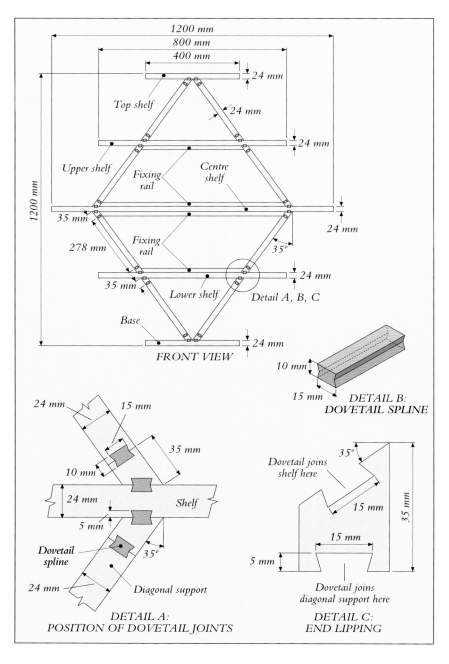

1200 mm
800 mm
400 mm
24 mm

Top shelf

24 mm

24 mm

Upper shelf

Fixing rail

Centre shelf

1200 mm

35 mm

24 mm

278 mm

Fixing rail

35°

35 mm

24 mm

Lower shelf

Detail A, B, C

Base

24 mm

FRONT VIEW

10 mm

15 mm

DETAIL B:
DOVETAIL SPLINE

24 mm   15 mm

35 mm

10 mm

24 mm   Shelf

5 mm

Dovetail spline

35°

24 mm   Diagonal support

DETAIL A:
POSITION OF DOVETAIL JOINTS

35°

Dovetail joins shelf here

15 mm

35 mm

15 mm

5 mm

Dovetail joins diagonal support here

DETAIL C:
END LIPPING

a 5 mm deep dovetail housing, exactly in the centre of the end of the board. Run dovetails on the eight diagonal supports.

MAKING THE END LIPPINGS
9 Take the 41 x 24 mm timber and cut it into four 1050 mm lengths. With a protractor, set a sliding bevel to 35 degrees. Use the bevel to set the base of a power saw to this angle.

10 With a marking gauge or square, mark a line 35 mm along one face of a length. Clamp the piece to the bench. Set the rip guide on the saw to cut the angle slightly over width, then cut. Repeat for all four lengths.

11 Clamp one length edge up in a vice. Plane the angle back to the marked line. Repeat for all lengths.

12 With a marking gauge, make a line down the centre of the bevelled edge and over the ends of each piece. Rout a dovetail groove down the square edge of each piece, then move the fence to cut the groove down the centre of the bevelled edge.

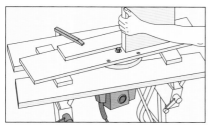

8 Set the router to cut a 5 mm deep dovetail housing, and run dovetails on the diagonal supports.

13 With a square, mark the lengths of the pieces to the same width as each diagonal support (225 mm). Score the lines with a utility knife and use a tenon saw to cut the pieces 1–2 mm over-length.

MAKING AND ATTACHING THE DOVETAIL SPLINES
14 Machine the 19 x 12 mm timber to a thickness of 10 mm, then cut it into eight 1050 mm lengths. Re-set the router fence and cut a dovetail pitch on the 10 mm edge. Turn the timber over and rout the other side (see diagram Detail B on page 27).

15 Machine the matching dovetail joints on the opposite squared edge. Ensure a good slide fit by gradually reducing the width with a number of passes over the router.

16 Cut thirty-two dovetail splines, each 227 mm long. Using a paintbrush, glue all dovetail grooves in the diagonal supports and the matching end lippings. Insert a spline in each diagonal support joint, attach the lippings, then clamp. The ends of the lippings and dovetail splines will overhang the supports at each end. Remove excess adhesive with a damp cloth, then leave to dry. Don't put dovetail splines in the angled edge of the lippings at this stage.

MAKING THE SHELVES
17 Measure and mark the length of each shelf directly from your set-out. Square the lines across each face and

over the edges. Score the lines with a utility knife and cut the shelves to length with a panel or power saw.

18 Position each shelf on the set-out. Use a square to mark the centre line position of each dovetail joint across the appropriate face.

19 Clamp the top shelf and base to your bench, with centre lines aligned. Set up a fence parallel to one of the centre-line marks, set at the correct distance. With your router cutter centred on the centre line, machine 5 mm deep cuts. Repeat for the remaining shelves.

20 Check the fit of all pieces, then disassemble them. Plane the lipping and dovetail spline overhangs so they are flush with the diagonal supports. Sand all parts with 120 grit abrasive paper, then 180 grit. Clean up the rough-sawn ends of each shelf.

FINAL ASSEMBLY AND INSTALLATION

21 Assemble the unit on the set-out. Take the top shelf and glue the two

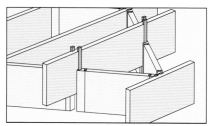

21 Fasten dovetail splines into the shelf dovetails, then fix the shelf into the diagonal support dovetails.

shelf dovetails and both ends of two dovetail splines. Next, glue the angled-edge dovetails in the diagonal supports. Fasten the dovetail splines into the shelf dovetails, then fix the shelf into the diagonal support dovetails. Repeat for all shelves.

22 Cut the 3000 mm length of light timber to make four fixing rails. Set up a sliding bevel at 35 degrees and cut the ends of the rails at this angle with a tenon saw, to fit flush against the inside edge of the supports.

23 Lay the unit front-side down and attach the rails to the shelves (see the diagram on page 27). Drill 5 mm holes and countersink, then fasten the rails with 40 mm x no. 8 cross-head screws. Finish the unit with clear lacquer.

24 To fix the unit to a framed wall, find the stud centres and mark them on the wall at the required height. Support the unit at this height (you may need help), and transfer the wall marks to the fixing rail. Drill and countersink a 5 mm clearance hole, then drill a 3 mm pilot hole. Attach the unit on one side first, with a 75 x no. 10 countersunk screw. Check the level with a spirit level, then drill and screw at the other end.

25 For a masonry wall, use a similar method and the same size screws. You will also need to insert a wall plug into the hole, into which you can fasten the screw.

This versatile shelving arrangement comprises a generous number of adjustable shelves and a feature shelf of contrasting cedar. The kicker and decorative top are made of solid silver ash.

Built-in shelving

These shelves allow you to maximize storage space in an awkwardly shaped spot. Instructions are given for units of equal width, but the specifications can easily be adapted – the example opposite features two top units, one on either side of a window.

TOOLS

- Tape measure or rule
- Combination square
- Pencil
- Pair of safety glasses
- Dust mask
- Hearing protection
- Panel saw or portable circular saw
- Coping saw
- Smoothing plane, jack plane or power plane

- Chisel: 25 mm
- Crowbar (optional)
- Portable electric drill
- Drill bits: 3 mm, 5 mm, countersink
- Screwdriver
- Spirit level
- Six G-cramps
- Eight 600 mm sash cramps

- Electric router (optional)
- Router bit: 19 mm bullnose cutter
- Spokeshave (optional)
- Old iron
- Cork sanding block
- Orbital sander (optional)

PREPARATION
1 Measure the area to find the exact lengths of timber required.

2 If you retain skirting boards and architraves, the units must be fastened to fixing blocks screwed to the skirtings and wall. If you want to remove a skirting, start at an external corner or join in the skirting. Lever the board out with a chisel until you can fit a crowbar behind it to prise it from the wall (a timber block between the bar and wall will protect the wall). On hollow walls, lever against the wall frame. Remove any nails and patch the plaster. To remove an architrave, drive a chisel into the joint between the architrave and jamb (do not chisel between the wall lining and architrave). Place scrap timber between the chisel and jamb, and lever off the architrave. Remove or drive in any nails, sand the jamb edge and fill the holes.

CUTTING OUT
3 Lay the chipboard and timber on a bench, and mark out the parts with a tape measure and square, checking that they are square and straight.

4 Wearing safety glasses, cut the parts with a panel saw or circular saw, then

MATERIALS★

PART	MATERIAL	FINISHED LENGTH	WIDTH	No.
Kicker front/ back panel	18 mm veneered chipboard	2630 mm	100 mm	2
Kicker rail/ end panel	18 mm veneered chipboard	250 mm	100 mm	6
Kicker face	125 x 25 mm light timber PAR	2710 mm		1
Base unit feature shelf☆	200 x 50 mm dark timber PAR	2730 mm		1
Base unit top/ bottom panel★★	18 mm veneered chipboard	2630 mm	316 mm	2
Base unit divider/ end panel★★	18 mm veneered chipboard	668 mm	316 mm	6
Base unit fill piece	18 mm veneered chipboard	668 mm	40 mm	2
Base unit back☆☆	12 mm veneered chipboard	668 mm	1053 mm	2
Base unit back☆☆	12 mm veneered chipboard	668 mm	523 mm	1
Base unit shelf☆	18 mm veneered chipboard	502 mm	315 mm	5
Top unit top panel★★	18 mm veneered chipboard	2594 mm	210 mm	1
Top unit divider★★	18 mm veneered chipboard	1892 mm	210 mm	4
Top unit end panel★★	18 mm veneered chipboard	1892 mm	215 mm	2
Top unit fill piece	18 mm veneered chipboard	1910 mm	40 mm	2
Top unit back☆☆	12 mm veneered chipboard	1910 mm	1053 mm	2
Top unit back☆☆	12 mm veneered chipboard	1910 mm	523 mm	1
Top unit shelf★★	18 mm veneered chipboard	502 mm	214 mm	30

MATERIALS★

Part	Material	Finished length	Width	No.
Decorative top	250 x 50 mm light timber PAR	2730 mm		1

OTHER: Twenty 50 mm x no. 8 countersunk screws; eighty 40 mm x no. 8 countersunk screws; twenty 28 mm x no. 8 countersunk screws; 5 mm shelf supports; abrasive paper: ten sheets of 180 grit, six sheets of 240 grit and two sheets of 120 grit; PVA adhesive; cloths; clear lacquer

★Overall finished size of units: 2740 mm high; 2710 mm wide. Top unit is 235 mm deep with decorative top; base unit is 350 mm deep with feature shelf. Timber sizes given are nominal. For timber types and sizes see page 64.
★★With one long edge of matching pre-glued edging.
*Made from two pieces of edge-jointed timber.
**Back pieces to be joined.

lightly plane the timber pieces. Check edges and faces for accuracy.

5 Glue matching veneer edging to any raw chipboard facing edges (see step 3 on page 54 for instructions). A timber merchant may also be able to cut and edge the pieces.

KICKER ASSEMBLY
6 Lay the kicker front and back panels side by side. Mark 18 mm in from either end of both panels, and square a line across (see the diagram on page 35). Mark the panel into five sections of equal width between the marked 18 mm positions. On each division, drill 5 mm holes, 25 mm in from the front and back edges.

7 Align the rails with the lines on the front and back panels and drill 3 mm pilot holes in each rail end. Fix the rails to the panels with 40 mm x no. 8 countersunk screws.

8 Check that the kicker is level using a spirit level. Fasten to fixing blocks screwed along the skirting board.

9 Attach the kicker face, which should be 18 mm thick x 100 mm wide, from inside the front panel. Drill 5 mm holes and fasten with 28 mm x no. 8 countersunk screws.

BASE UNIT ASSEMBLY
10 Sand all remaining components, starting with 180 grit abrasive paper and finishing with 240 grit.

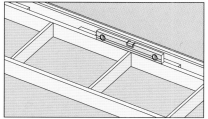

8 Check that the kicker is level, then fasten it to fixing blocks screwed along the skirting board.

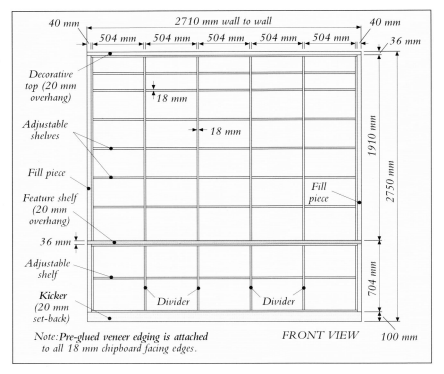

40 mm

2710 mm wall to wall

40 mm

504 mm | 504 mm | 504 mm | 504 mm | 504 mm

36 mm

Decorative
top (20 mm
overhang)

18 mm

Adjustable
shelves

18 mm

1910 mm

Fill piece

Fill
piece

Feature shelf
(20 mm
overhang)

2750 mm

36 mm

Adjustable
shelf

Kicker
(20 mm
set-back)

Divider

Divider

704 mm

Note: Pre-glued veneer edging is attached
to all 18 mm chipboard facing edges.

FRONT VIEW

100 mm

11 Place the top and bottom panels of the base unit edge to edge, best faces up. Mark 18 mm in from either end of both panels. Square a line across and divide each panel into five sections as in step 6. On the end division, drill two 5 mm holes, 30 mm in from the front and back edges, and a central hole. Make a drilling template from scrap chipboard for positioning the adjustable shelf pins. The holes can be 30–50 mm apart.

12 Place the left-hand end and bottom panels on the bench, face edges up. Glue the joining end of the end panel and align it flush with the

end of the bottom panel. Drill 3 mm pilot holes and fasten with 40 mm x no. 8 countersunk screws. Repeat this step for the opposite end.

13 Make a spacer block to suit the divider spacings. Put the spacer hard against the end. Glue the end of the divider and fasten as in step 12. Repeat to attach all dividers to the bottom panel. Turn the unit upright and fasten the top in the same way. Remove excess adhesive.

14 Place the unit on the bench, face up. Sand all edges – if available, use an orbital sander over all surfaces for

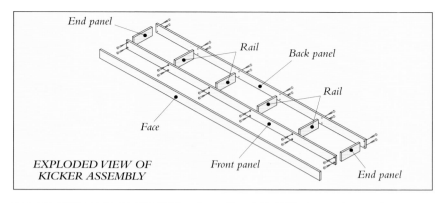

End panel
Rail
Back panel
Rail
Face
Front panel
End panel

**EXPLODED VIEW OF
KICKER ASSEMBLY**

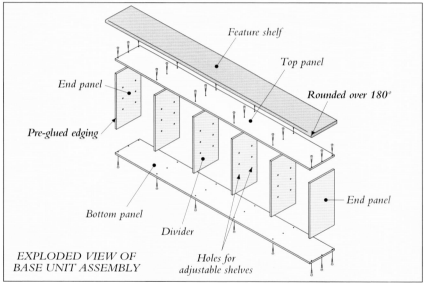

Feature shelf
Top panel
End panel
Rounded over 180°
Pre-glued edging
Bottom panel
Divider
End panel
Holes for
adjustable shelves

**EXPLODED VIEW OF
BASE UNIT ASSEMBLY**

a smooth finish. Check that the backs are square. After sanding, lay the backs on the unit, face side down: the two large backs should be to the outside, the narrow back should be positioned between them. The back panels should join over a divider. Drill 3 mm pilot holes, 250 mm apart, all around the back edge of the

unit and the back pieces. Stagger the screw holes over the dividers. Drill 5 mm holes and countersink, then attach the back using 28 mm x no. 8 countersunk screws.

15 Apply clear lacquer to the unit before installation. Cut two fill pieces the height of the base unit and plane

to the width of the gap between the wall and the unit. With a coping saw, make a cut-out to fit around the skirting board. Use adhesive and two 40 mm nails inserted from inside the base unit to fasten the pieces. Punch in and fill the nail heads, sand back, then touch up with lacquer.

FEATURE SHELF ASSEMBLY

16 Take the two timber feature shelf pieces and plane and joint them straight and square. The finished shelf should be 36 mm thick x 350 mm wide. Glue the joining edges, hold them together with sash cramps and remove excess adhesive. Ensure that top joints are flush, and leave to dry.

17 Use a plane, spokeshave or roundover bit in a router to round over the front edge of the shelf.

18 Sand the shelf with 240 grit abrasive paper, apply matching filler, and finish with clear lacquer

TOP UNIT ASSEMBLY

19 Take the top unit end panels and dividers, and mark adjustable shelf

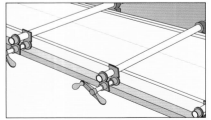

16 Glue both joining edges and place them within sash cramps, then immediately remove excess adhesive.

positions. Drill 5 mm holes for the shelves, 35 mm in from the front and back edges, starting 40 mm up from the bottom of the panels.

20 The feature shelf acts as the bottom panel for the top unit. Set out the placement of dividers and end panels from a squared line across the bottom of the shelf. From this centre line measure half the division distance each side of the centre, then 18 mm, then the full division distance, until all the spaces have been marked. Fit the feature shelf to the wall very carefully at the front of each end and to 150 mm back from the front edge. The area beyond will be hidden by the top unit filler pieces.

21 Mark 18 mm in from each end of the top panel. Square a line across and divide each panel into five sections as in step 6. On each divider, drill 5 mm holes, 40 mm in from both the front and back edges.

22 Lay the left-hand end panel and top panel on their back edges. Glue joining edges, clamp in position, and fasten with 40 mm x no. 8 counter-sunk screws. Do the same to fix dividers and the other end panel to the top panel. Align the feature shelf and dividers and fasten with two 60 mm x no. 8 countersunk screws at each divider.

TOP UNIT INSTALLATION

23 Slide the top unit into position on the base unit. Fasten it with

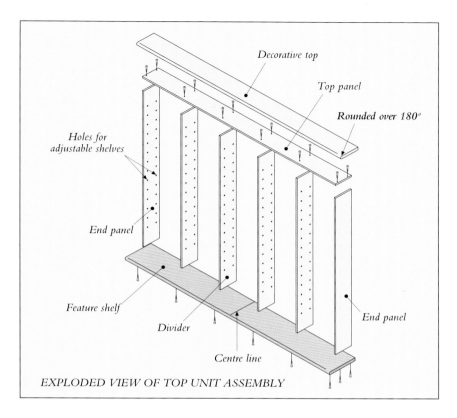

Decorative top

Top panel

Rounded over 180°

Holes for adjustable shelves

End panel

Feature shelf

Divider

End panel

Centre line

EXPLODED VIEW OF TOP UNIT ASSEMBLY

28 mm x no. 8 countersunk screws, screwing through the top panel of the base unit into the feature shelf. Use a 5 mm clearance hole and countersink the screw holes so the screws finish flush.

24 Measure the gap between the wall and the unit on the sides, bottom, middle and top. Mark the measurements on the faces of the fill pieces and use a steel rule to join the marks. Plane down to the line and fit the fill pieces to the gaps. Fasten to the wall.

25 The finished decorative top should be 36 mm thick x 235 mm wide. Round over the front edge of the top, then cut it to the correct length. Use 50 mm x no. 8 countersunk screws to fasten it to the top of the unit from above.

26 Fill holes and repair any damage. Sand all parts, including adjustable shelves, with 240 grit abrasive paper, and finish with lacquer.

27 Place shelf supports in the prepared holes and insert the shelves.

Small turntable bookcase

This ingenious unit is ideal for storing paperbacks and other small books. It is mounted on a swivelling base, providing access from all four sides.

TOOLS

- Tape measure or steel rule
- Combination square
- Marking gauge
- Pencil
- Pair of safety glasses
- Dust mask
- Hearing protection
- Smoothing plane or jack plane
- Panel saw or circular saw
- Tenon saw
- Mitre saw (optional)

- Electric jigsaw or coping saw
- Mitre box (optional)
- Dowelling jig with 6 mm bush
- Electric router
- Router bit: 19 mm straight
- Electric drill
- Drill bits: 3 mm, 4 mm, 6 mm, countersink
- Chisel: 16 mm, bevelled edges
- Utility knife

- Four 600 mm sash cramps
- Six G-cramps
- Cork sanding block or timber 19 mm thick x 110 long x 70 mm wide
- Hammer or mallet
- Screwdriver
- Vice
- Flat-bottomed spokeshave
- Compass

CUTTING OUT

1 To save time, get a timber supplier to plane the timber on all faces.

2 Lay the 175 x 25 mm timber on the bench and measure, mark and cut two pieces 920 mm long. These will be edge-jointed to make a wide board, from which the top, base and long divider will later be cut.

3 Mark best faces. Check that each piece is straight and square with a combination square. Ensure that joining edges can be clamped up tightly, adjusting with a smoothing or jack plane. Hold the two lengths edge to edge with the ends flush. Mark the lengths of the top, base and the long divider, allowing for saw cuts and cleaning up. Square the lines around all faces of each piece.

4 With a marking gauge mark a centre line down the middle of each joining edge. Clamp boards face side together so the length lines align. Find the centre of each component along the edge. Measure 100 mm each side of the centre and square the

The top and base of this bookcase are made from two pieces of timber joined almost invisibly by a dowelled joint. A strip of dark teak inlay makes an effective contrast with the rock maple used for the rest of the unit.

MATERIALS★

Part	Material	Finished length	No.
Top★★	175 x 25 mm light timber PAR	300 mm	2
Top lipping☆	38 x 25 mm light timber PAR	1500 mm	1
Inlay☆	7 x 25 mm dark timber PAR	1500 mm	1
Long divider★★	175 x 25 mm light timber PAR	280 mm	2
Short divider	175 x 25 mm light timber PAR	280 mm	2
Vertical support	25 x 25 mm light timber PAR	270 mm	4
Base★★	175 x 25 mm light timber PAR	300 mm	2
Base lipping☆	75 x 25 mm light timber PAR	1500 mm	1
Turntable base	18 mm MDF	295 x 295 mm	2

OTHER: Fourteen 6 x 30 mm dowels for exterior supports; PVA adhesive; cloths; scrap board 16 mm thick, 400 mm long, 120 mm wide; abrasive paper: three sheets of 120 grit, three sheets of 180 grit and two sheets of 240 grit; eight 12 mm x no. 8 panhead self-tapping screws; one 'lazy susan' swivel; finish of your choice.

★Finished size: 357 mm high; 352 mm wide. For timber types and sizes see page 64. Timber sizes given are nominal.
★★To be cut from two edge-jointed timber pieces.
☆To be mitred into four pieces.

lines across and over edges and faces. Mark six dowel holes on each edge.

5 Use a dowelling jig and 6 mm drill bit to bore 16 mm deep dowel holes.

6 Place the boards in two loosened sash cramps. Use a pencil to spread PVA adhesive in the dowel holes and across the face edges, and to remove any excess adhesive. Insert 6 x 30 mm dowels in the holes in one board and gently hammer in. Position the dowels against the holes in the opposite board, then push the boards together. If necessary, tap them with a hammer and block. Tighten the cramps, then attach two

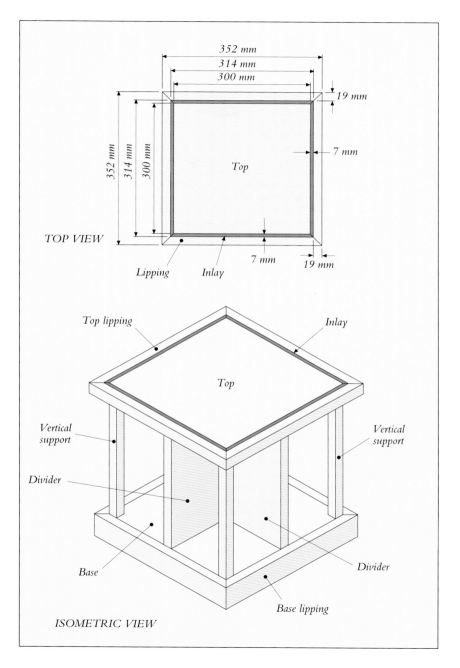

TOP VIEW

352 mm
314 mm
300 mm
19 mm
7 mm
Top
352 mm
314 mm
300 mm
Lipping   Inlay
7 mm
19 mm

ISOMETRIC VIEW

Top lipping
Inlay
Top
Vertical support
Vertical support
Divider
Base
Divider
Base lipping

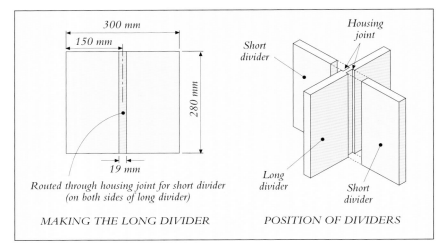

300 mm

150 mm

280 mm

19 mm

*Routed through housing joint for short divider
(on both sides of long divider)*

MAKING THE LONG DIVIDER

Short
divider

Housing
joint

Long
divider

Short
divider

POSITION OF DIVIDERS

extra sash cramps. Remove excess adhesive with a damp cloth. When dry, check for twist, bowing or cupping. Plane to adjust them.

MAKING THE TOP AND BASE

7 Cut out the 300 x 300 x 19 mm top and base pieces from the joined piece. Use a square and utility knife to cut cross-grain fibres, then cut the lengths to size with a panel saw or circular saw. Plane edges and ends square and straight back to your

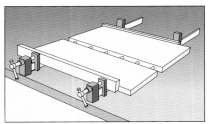

6 Place the boards within two loosened sash cramps. Insert dowels, then push the boards together.

marks. Plane the end grain from each side towards the centre to form a 'hill', then plane the hill flat.

8 Place the top piece best face down. Find the centre and mark a line square to one side. Measure out 9.5 mm either side of the centre and mark a line. Turn the board through 90 degrees and do the same again.

9 If routing the through housings, clamp a 400 x 120 x 16 mm fence to the top piece (see page 11 for notes on using a router). Attach a 19 mm bit, set to cut 5 mm deep. Set up the router on the marks and cut right through them, running the base plate firmly along the fence. Alternatively, use a tenon saw and chisel. Repeat steps 8 and 9 for the base piece.

MAKING THE DIVIDERS

10 The timber for the long divider should measure 280 x 300 x 19 mm.

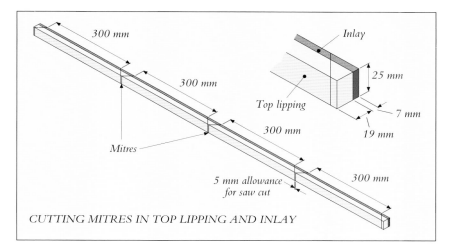

CUTTING MITRES IN TOP LIPPING AND INLAY

Use a ruler to measure in 150 mm from one end and mark a line straight across to the opposite side. Measure out 9.5 mm from either side of this line and mark lines down to the opposite end. Turn the divider over and repeat the process. Using a router with a 19 mm cutter, or a tenon saw and chisel, cut a through housing 5 mm deep. Turn the divider over and repeat the process.

11 The two short dividers must measure 280 x 146 x 19 mm. Check that the long and short dividers fit together and in the top and base piece housing joints. Flush the divider edges to the top and base pieces and number each joint.

MAKING THE BASE LIPPING
12 Mark a 45-degree line at one end of the base lipping and measure along 300 mm from the inside edge. Mark a 45-degree line at the measurement.

Square a line across each side, allowing 5 mm for saw cuts. Score the mitre lines with a utility knife. Mark three more mitred sections the same way.

13 Use a mitre box and fine-toothed saw to cut the mitres. Position the four lengths together and adjust the fit by planing. Use a smoothing plane to smooth the mitres if necessary.

14 Glue the joining edges of the mitred lipping to the base. Attach

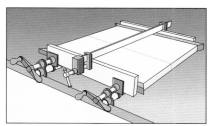

14 Glue the joining edges. Clamp the base and lipping together with sash cramps, and leave to dry.

lippings to the opposite base edges first. Clamp the base and lippings together with sash cramps, remove excess adhesive, and leave to dry. Then fit the remaining two lippings.

MAKING THE INLAY AND TOP LIPPING

15 Take the inlay strip, which should be 19 mm wide and 7 mm thick, and glue it to the top lipping. Clamp the inlay and lipping together with G-cramps, remove any excess adhesive, and allow to dry.

16 Mitre the joined lipping and inlay into four pieces using the process described in steps 12 and 13 (see the diagram on page 43).

17 Plane the mitre edges, then glue one mitred piece to one edge of the top piece. Clamp with sash cramps and leave to dry. Repeat for each mitred piece. Sand or plane the lippings flush with the base and top.

FINAL ASSEMBLY

18 Take the top and base pieces and mark dowel positions for the vertical

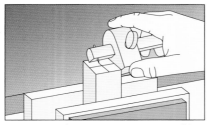

19 For each support, use a marking gauge set at 9.5 mm to find and mark the centre of the end faces.

Supports are fastened with dowels, and dividers are held in place by through housing joints.

supports. Set a marking gauge to 9.5 mm and mark a line from each corner of the top of the base piece (see the diagram on page 45). Repeat this marking process for the underside of the top piece. Drill 6 mm holes to a depth of 12 mm at the point where the marked lines intersect at each corner.

19 For each support, use a marking gauge set at 9.5 mm to find and mark the centre of the end faces. With a dowelling jig and a drill and twist bit, bore 6 mm holes 22 mm deep at the centre of each support.

20 Sand all parts with 120, 180 and 220 grit abrasive paper. Glue the dowel holes in the supports and tap in dowels. Next, glue the base piece housing joints. Insert the long divider and two short dividers, which have been glued along the bottom edges.

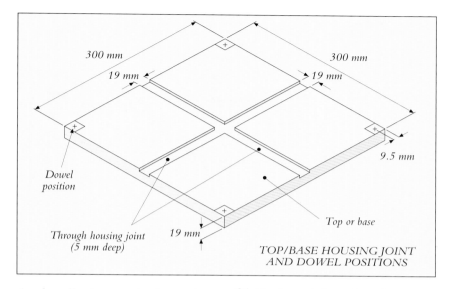

300 mm

300 mm

19 mm

19 mm

9.5 mm

Dowel
position

Top or base

Through housing joint
(5 mm deep)

19 mm

*TOP/BASE HOUSING JOINT
AND DOWEL POSITIONS*

Apply adhesive to the base piece dowel holes and insert vertical supports and their dowels. Take the top piece and glue the dowel holes and housing joints as you did for the base. Insert the glued dividers into the housing joints—the short dividers slot into the housings in the long divider. Fix the dowelled supports into the dowel holes. Clamp with four sash cramps, clean off excess adhesive, and leave to dry.

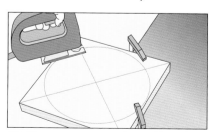

**22 Use a compass and pencil to draw
a 290 mm diameter circle on one face.
Cut out with a jigsaw.**

21 Finely sand the unit with 180 grit abrasive paper and finish with 240 grit abrasive paper. Apply your chosen finish.

MAKING THE SWIVEL BASE
22 Glue and clamp the MDF pieces together. When dry, mark the centre and use a compass and pencil to draw a 290 mm diameter circle on one face. Wearing a dust mask and safety glasses, cut out the circle with a jigsaw or coping saw. Clean up the edges using 120 grit abrasive paper or a flat-bottomed spokeshave.

23 Fit the 'lazy susan' between the bookcase and swivel base following the manufacturer's instructions. 'Lazy susan' swivels come in many sizes. For best results use one no larger in diameter than 300 mm and no smaller than 200 mm.

This unit is more than a simple bookcase — with its pull-out desk it also serves as a tiny office or library area. The decorative mouldings shown here are made from chamfered and fluted maple, but moulded skirtings can also be used.

Bookcase with pull-out desk

One of these two joined units contains a writing desk, which pulls out and rises to the level of the shelf proper by means of an ingenious system of pins and grooves. This project requires experience in using a router.

TOOLS

- Tape measure
- Combination square
- Pencil
- Pair of safety glasses
- Dust mask
- Hearing protection
- Tenon saw
- Panel saw or circular saw)
- Jigsaw
- Electric router

- Router bit: 5 mm and 18 mm straight
- Six G-cramps
- Six 900 mm sash cramps
- Vice
- Electric drill
- Drill bits: 8 mm, 5 mm, 3 mm, countersink
- Plane

- Dowelling jig (optional)
- Small paintbrush (optional)
- Screwdriver (cross-head or slotted)
- Half-round wood rasp or half-round file
- Hammer
- Cork sanding block
- Straight-edge

CUTTING OUT

1 Lay the MDF on a bench. Mark out the parts using a tape measure and square.

2 Wearing safety glasses and a dust mask, cut parts slightly oversize with a panel saw or circular saw. Trim edges back with a router. A timber supplier could cut the MDF to size.

MAKING THE HOUSINGS AND REBATE

3 Use a guide fence clamped to the face of the boards or make a router jig with the threaded rod and nuts.

4 Attach it to the router, 82 mm away from the 18 mm cutter, and set the cutter depth to 6 mm. Take one of the end panels and rout the first stopped housing for the shelves,

4 Turn the fence over and set the distance to 300 mm. Start from the back edge and rout to the front.

MATERIALS*

Part	Material	Length	Width	No.
End panel	18 mm MDF	2000 mm	300 mm	4
Shelf	18 mm MDF	775 mm	296 mm	11
Rail	18 mm MDF	764 mm	82 mm	4
Shelf (sliding)	18 mm MDF	760 mm	200 mm	1
Back	4 mm MDF	1836 mm	787 mm	2
Side moulding	50 x 25 mm softwood PAR	319 mm		3
Front moulding (top)★★	50 x 25 mm softwood PAR	1639 mm		1
Front moulding (bottom)★★	50 x 25 mm softwood PAR	838 mm		1
Loper☆	50 x 25 mm hardwood PAR	600 mm		1
Glue block	50 x 50 mm softwood PAR	200 mm		12

OTHER: PVA adhesive; cloths; sixteen 40 mm long, 8 mm diameter timber dowels; abrasive paper: three sheets of 120 grit and three sheets of 180 grit; four 40 mm x no. 8 countersunk screws; eighteen 30 mm x no. 6 countersunk screws; 30 mm panel pins; two 50 x 6 mm coach bolts with washers and wing nuts; sixteen 30 mm lost-head nails; 25 mm flat-head nails; four 12 x 5 mm diameter steel guide pins; finish of your choice.
For the jig: Two lengths of threaded rod 600 mm long and four nuts to suit.

*Finished size of each unit: 2000 mm high; 800 mm wide without moulding; the shelves are 295 mm deep. When opened out the desk-shelf is approximately 500 mm deep. For timber types and timber sizes see page 64. Timber sizes given here are nominal.
★★Commercial moulding 100 x 25 mm (finished size 91 x 19 mm) can be used instead of timber.
☆To be cut later to make two lopers.

stopping 10 mm in from the front edge. Repeat this process on all the end panels. Turn the fence over and set the distance to 300 mm. Do not change the cutter depth. Ensure that the fence fits neatly into the first housing and that it slides easily (if it doesn't, adjust by shaving a fraction off the side of the fence until it slides without sticking). Start from the back edge and rout to the front edge, repeating the process to make the right number of cuts on the right-hand end panels. Swap the fence to

A system of pins in routed slots allows the desk to pull out and lift up to the level of the shelf behind.

the other side of the router for the left-hand ends.

5 Now rebate the back edges. Pair off the end panels, and on the inside face use a pencil to mark the back edges with a cross. Replace the jig with the normal fence and set the router to cut to a depth of 12.5 mm and to a width of 4.5 mm. Rout rebates on the inside back edge of the end panels.

ROUTING THE DESK TRACK AND SHELF STOPS

6 Before routing the sliding track for the desk with a 5 mm straight cutter, carefully set the grooves out on the end panels (see the diagram Detail A on page 51). Take a pair of ends and measure the distance from the cutting edge of the router bit to the outer edge of the router base. Set the bit to cut 9 mm deep. At the measured distance from the marked groove, clamp on a piece of off cut, to act as a fence.

7 Use a square to mark the positions of the angled cut and the fence. With the fence on the right, push the router away from you. Drill 5 mm holes for the guide pins.

8 Take the 600 x 50 x 25 mm timber and set out the grooves working from each end so that the grooves form a pair (see the diagram Detail B on page 51). Clamp the timber to the bench and then run the fence along one edge. Next, rout the two long grooves. To cut the short grooves parallel to the long ones, re-attach the

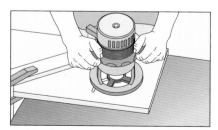

7 Mark the angled cut and fence positions. With the fence on the right, push the router away from you.

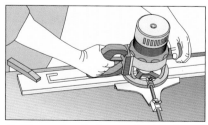

8 Clamp the timber to the bench and run the fence along one edge. Rout the long grooves.

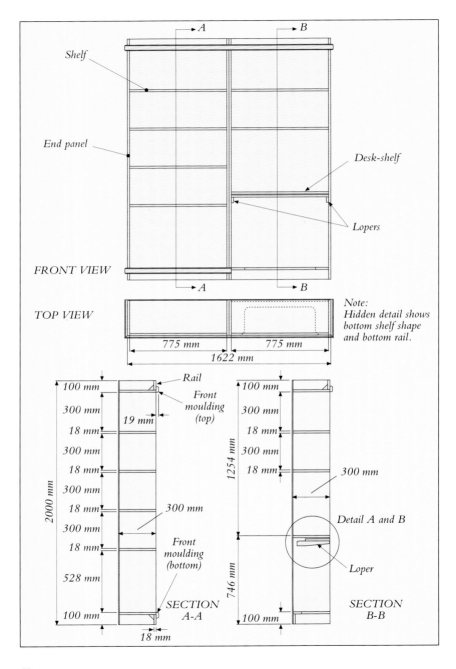

A ▶   B ▶

Shelf

End panel

Desk-shelf

Lopers

FRONT VIEW
▶ A   ▶ B

TOP VIEW

Note:
Hidden detail shows
bottom shelf shape
and bottom rail.

775 mm   775 mm
1622 mm

Rail
Front
moulding
(top)

100 mm
300 mm
18 mm
300 mm
19 mm
18 mm
300 mm
300 mm
18 mm
300 mm
18 mm
528 mm

2000 mm

Front
moulding
(bottom)

100 mm

SECTION
A-A

18 mm

100 mm
300 mm
18 mm
300 mm
18 mm

1254 mm

300 mm

Detail A and B

Loper

746 mm

100 mm

SECTION
B-B

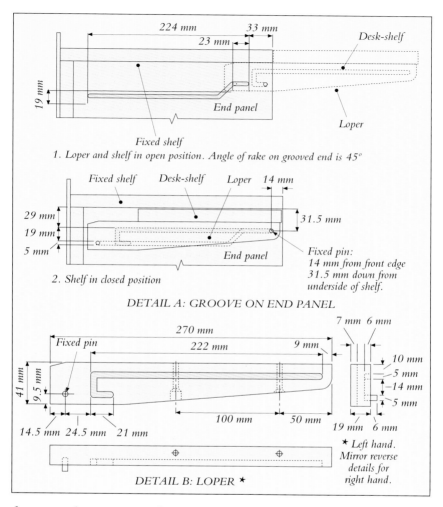

1. Loper and shelf in open position. Angle of rake on grooved end is 45°

2. Shelf in closed position

Fixed pin:
14 mm from front edge
31.5 mm down from
underside of shelf.

DETAIL A: GROOVE ON END PANEL

DETAIL B: LOPER ★

★ Left hand.
Mirror reverse
details for
right hand.

fence to the router and set the distances before cutting.

9 Cut the piece in half to separate the lopers and line up the two end grooves with a square. Clamp the pieces with a length of off cut as a fence, and rout the groove. Place the lopers with faces together in a vice

and plane the edges to the bevel indicated. Drill and counterbore two screw holes on each loper (see the diagram above) and two 5 mm holes for the guide pins.

10 Clamp the shelves together, with all the ends square and flush. Rout stops 19 mm deep and 6 mm wide.

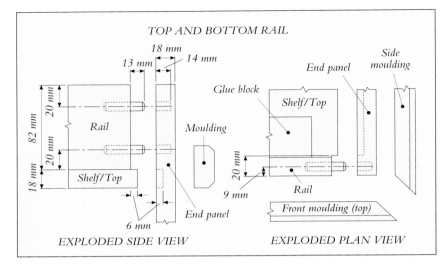

TOP AND BOTTOM RAIL

EXPLODED SIDE VIEW

EXPLODED PLAN VIEW

FIXING THE RAILS

11 Rails are placed at the top front edges of both units, the bottom front of the large unit and the bottom back of the desk unit. Mark out dowel hole positions on the rails, 20 mm in from the top and bottom and in the centre of the rail end. Use a square to mark corresponding hole positions on the end panel. Place the rails together in a vice, with all ends flush. Use a dowelling jig and a drill and twist bit to bore 8 mm x 31 mm deep holes in the rail ends. Drill 11 mm deep holes in the end panels.

ASSEMBLING THE UNIT

12 Use a small paintbrush to glue the housing grooves on one end first. Spread adhesive into the dowel holes with a pencil. Insert dowels, rails and shelves and tap them in using a scrap block. Glue the other end panel and locate it on the assembled parts.

13 Nail or screw the unit together or clamp it overnight. If the housing joints are a little loose, they should be nailed and glued. If very loose, they should be screwed using a 40 mm countersunk screw with a clearance hole and pilot hole 50 mm back from the front edge and 50 mm from the back edge. If the unit is nailed or screwed you can work on it half an hour after gluing, but you will have to fill the heads and sand them back at a later stage. Apply glue blocks behind the rails.

14 Measure from the inside face of each end panel 100 mm along the bottom shelf. Square a line from front to back at this point.

15 With a marking gauge, mark a line parallel to the back edge and 60 mm in. Set a compass to 40 mm and inscribe the curved corners of

the cut-out on to the bottom shelf. Use a jigsaw to remove the waste. Clean up the rough saw marks with a half-round wood rasp or file, finishing the curves with 120 grit abrasive paper.

16 Check that the backs fit, but do not fix them on. To temporarily keep the units square, tack an off cut of backing material diagonally across the corners and place shrinkage plates across the bottom of each end panel.

17 For the trim use chamfered and fluted timber or a moulded skirting. Mark out the mitres with a square, cut them, then cut the mouldings to length. Clamp them to the unit and fix to the sides with adhesive and 30 mm panel pins, first checking that they are square to the face edges (or fasten from inside the rail, using 30 mm x no. 6 countersunk screws). Place the bottom front moulding over the mitred side piece and mark the length at the opposite end. It should overlap the front edge of the other unit 18 mm. Cut to length and fit. Don't fix the top moulding.

18 Lay the large unit on its side. Put the desk unit on its side on top of the large unit and align the front and top edges. Drill two 6.5 mm holes through both end panels where they won't be seen, 150–200 mm apart. They will take two 50 x 6 mm coach bolts with washers and nuts. Drill and countersink four 4 mm holes for four 30 mm x no. 6 screws further

down the end. Place two holes below the second shelf, one near each front and back edge, and two above the bottom shelf (these two must be accessible after assembly).

FINISHING

19 Sand the edges of each piece with 120 grit paper, finishing with 180 grit. Do not sand the MDF faces. Finish as desired.

20 Lay the units face down on padded bearers to protect the faces. Remove the braces. Mark the shelf centre-line positions on the back edge so you can locate them when the back is in place. Position the back flush with the top edge and fasten with 25 mm flat-head nails. Use a straight-edge and pencil to draw a line across the back where the shelves will be nailed, then nail them down. Repeat for the other unit.

21 Turn the desk unit upside down. Drop in the shelf and bring it to within 1 mm of the front edge. Ensure the gaps on each side are equal and lightly clamp it in position. Insert guide pins in the ends and lopers. Position the lopers flush with the front edge and sides of the shelf, and attach with 40 mm x no. 8 countersunk screws. Don't glue lopers: they may need to be replaced.

22 Stand the shelf unit in position, align the desk unit and fasten with nuts, bolts and screws. Glue and nail the top front moulding in place.

Modular units with optional doors

These sleek units can be used as open shelving, or two glass doors can be attached to each unit. This project provides an opportunity to perfect a variety of important basic techniques.

TOOLS

- Steel rule: 150 mm or 300 mm
- Tape measure
- Combination square
- Pencil
- Pair of safety glasses
- Dust mask
- Hearing protection
- Panel saw or circular saw
- Tenon saw
- Utility knife
- Vice

- Rebate plane
- Smoothing plane or jack plane
- Electric router
- Router bit: 18 mm straight
- Four G-cramps
- Six 800 mm sash cramps
- Marking gauge
- Mortise gauge
- Chisel: 16 mm, bevelled edges; 25 mm
- Smoothing file

- Round file
- Old iron
- Cork sanding block
- Belt sander (optional)
- Electric drill
- Drill bit: 3 mm, 5 mm, 6 mm, 10 mm countersink, 32 mm Forstner
- Dowelling jig with 6 mm bush
- Dowel stick (optional)
- Hammer
- Nail punch

CUTTING OUT

1 Lay the chipboard and timber on a workbench, and use a tape measure and square to mark out the parts, checking that each of them is square and straight.

2 Wearing safety glasses, cut the parts with a panel saw or circular saw, then lightly plane the timber. Use a square to check accuracy on all edges and faces. Label the pieces, and mark the face side and edges. A timber merchant may be able to cut the pieces and attach veneer edging.

3 Fix matching veneer edging to the raw chipboard edges as specified. Use an old iron at a hot setting. Hold the chipboard on its edge and position the veneer adhesive side down. Move the iron back and forth along the veneer, pressing it down ahead of the iron with a cork block. Clean up overhanging edge tape with a round file, then sand the edges and arris with 120 grit abrasive paper.

PREPARING END PANELS

4 Lay out the end panels in pairs (using best faces for the outer sides).

Without doors each unit is an easily accessible bookcase; with doors it becomes a secure display cabinet for your most valuable and beautiful books. The doors are made of solid silver ash, and the basic unit is veneered in matching timber.

MATERIALS*

PART	MATERIAL	LENGTH	WIDTH	NO.
End panel**	25 mm veneered chipboard	2100 mm	395 mm	6
Top/bottom/ centre panel**	25 mm veneered chipboard	510 mm	390 mm	9
Adjustable shelf**	25 mm veneered chipboard	498 mm	370 mm	12
Back	4 mm veneered chipboard	1980 mm	531 mm	3
Top rail and base kicker	25 mm veneered chipboard	500 mm	60 mm	6
Timber cleat (horizontal)	19 x 19 mm timber PAR	458 mm		6
Timber cleat (vertical)	19 x 19 mm timber PAR	59 mm		12
Door stile*	70 x 20 mm timber	951 mm		12
Door rail*	70 x 20 mm timber	378 mm		12
Door bead (vertical)*	9 x 9 mm timber	833 mm		12
Door bead (horizontal)*	9 x 9 mm timber	361 mm		12

OTHER (for three units): 150 of 25 mm flat-head nails (units and doors); four 5 mm supports for each shelf; twenty 8 mm brass sleeves for each shelf; twelve concealed hinges with 16 mm cranking; thirty 30 mm x no. 8 countersunk cross-head screws; eighty 15 mm panel pins; forty-eight 32 mm long x 6 mm diameter timber dowels; six sheets of pre-cut clear glass 829 mm long x 376 mm wide x 3 mm thick; abrasive paper: nine sheets of 180 grit and five sheets of 220 grit; finish of your choice; handles of your choice
For the jig: one piece 16 mm MDF 1800 x 850 mm; two pieces 12 mm MDF 1800 x 90 mm (with long edges laminated); one piece 16 mm MDF 850 x 120 mm (with long edges laminated); two 14 mm blocks 120 x 90 mm

*Quantity of materials based on building three units. Finished size of single unit: 2100 mm high; 550 wide; 396 mm deep. For timber types and timber sizes see page 64. Timber sizes given here are nominal unless otherwise indicated.
**With one long edge of matching timber veneer pre-glued edging.
*Finished size.

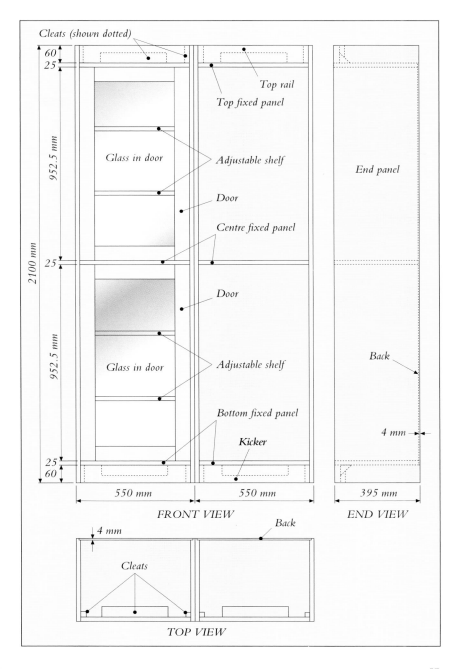

Cleats (shown dotted)

60
25

952.5 mm

2100 mm

25

952.5 mm

25
60

Top rail

Top fixed panel

Glass in door

Adjustable shelf

Door

Centre fixed panel

Door

Adjustable shelf

Glass in door

Bottom fixed panel

Kicker

End panel

Back

4 mm

550 mm   550 mm   395 mm

FRONT VIEW   END VIEW

4 mm   Back

Cleats

TOP VIEW

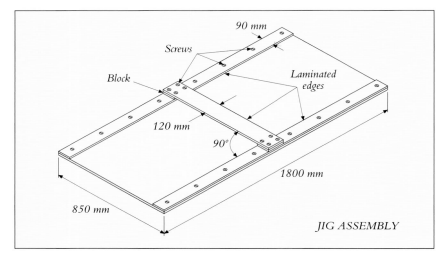

90 mm

Screws

Block

Laminated
edges

120 mm

90°

1800 mm

850 mm

JIG ASSEMBLY

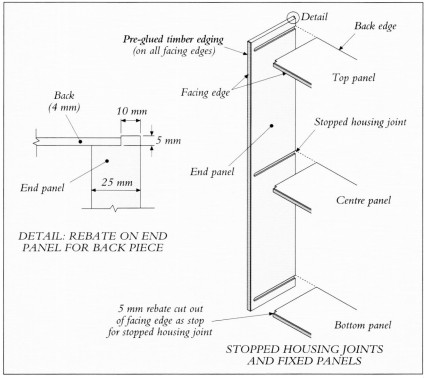

Detail

Back edge

Pre-glued timber edging
(on all facing edges)

Top panel

Back
(4 mm)

10 mm

Facing edge

5 mm

Stopped housing joint

End panel

End panel

25 mm

Centre panel

*DETAIL: REBATE ON END
PANEL FOR BACK PIECE*

5 mm rebate cut out
*of facing edge as stop
for stopped housing joint*

Bottom panel

*STOPPED HOUSING JOINTS
AND FIXED PANELS*

Cut a rebate 15 mm deep and 5 mm wide along the back inside edge of each panel, using a rebate plane or a router. If using the router, fit a fence and an 18 mm straight cutter (see page 11 for notes on using a router). The plywood back will be secured within this rebate at a later stage.

5 Before routing, build a jig (see the diagram opposite).

6 Mark the positions of the housing joints on the end panels. Leave 60 mm between the top of the end panel and the top joint, and 60 mm between the base of the panel and the bottom joint. The central joint should be an equal distance between the top and bottom joints.

7 Rout the joints. Slide each end panel into the jig and clamp with a G-cramp. Attach an 18 mm straight cutter set to cut 5 mm deep. Rout a 25 mm wide groove, leaving 10 mm uncut on the front edge. Make two passes for a width of 25 mm.

8 Mark and drill holes for adjustable shelves in the end panels. Bore 8 mm deep holes 60 mm in from the front and back edges, 32 mm apart.

PREPARING FIXED PANELS
9 Take one of the top fixed panels. On each end use a marking gauge set at 5 mm to mark a line right across the facing edge and in 15 mm on either side. Repeat for the other fixed panels.

10 Hold the top panel in a vice and use a tenon saw to cut out a 5 mm rebate as shown in the diagram on the opposite page. Repeat for the other fixed panels.

ASSEMBLING THE UNIT
11 Sand all the unit components with 180 grit abrasive paper.

12 Lay both end panels on the bench and glue the housing joints. Place the fixed panels into position, hold with sash cramps, then clean off excess adhesive and leave to dry.

13 Check that the back fits in the end panel rebates, cutting the back board to adjust the size if necessary. Fasten using 25 mm flat-head nails.

ATTACHING THE RAIL, KICKER AND CLEATS
14 Lay the unit on its back on the bench, ready for the top rail, kicker and cleats to be attached.

15 Place the top rail flat on its good face. On the back face, position a short vertical cleat at either end, flush

17 Slide each end panel into the jig and clamp it. Rout a groove, leaving 10 mm uncut on the front edge.

with the edge. Attach the long horizontal cleat along the bottom edge between the two short cleats.

16 Glue the cleats in place. Secure the short cleats with two evenly spaced screws each way, and the long cleat with six screws. Stagger the screws so they don't run into one another. Bore 3 mm pilot holes through the cleats into the rail. Drill 5 mm holes in the cleats only and countersink. Insert 30 mm x no. 8 countersunk cross-head screws and tighten. Wipe off excess adhesive. Repeat the process for the kicker, but attach cleats at the top edge.

17 Glue the edges of the top rail and kicker that will join the unit, and fix to the unit with sash cramps. Bore 3 mm pilot holes in the pieces at regular intervals, drill 5 mm holes, countersink, then insert 30 mm x no. 8 screws and tighten. Wipe off excess adhesive with a damp cloth. Apply the finish of your choice. Insert brass sleeves in the shelf holes, and position shelves now if you are not adding doors.

MAKING DOWELLED JOINTS FOR THE DOORS

18 Use a rebate plane or a router for the following step. If using a router, set it up with an 18 mm bit to cut 14 mm deep and 10 mm wide. Clamp all stiles and rails to the bench with G-cramps and cut out one long edge along each piece. Glass panels will sit within these rebated edges.

19 Set the marking gauge to 10 mm and mark a line on the facing edge of the rails. Using a square and utility knife, score along the marked line.

20 Place each rail in a vice. On the front edge of the end that will meet the stile, cut a 10 x 6 mm rebate with a tenon saw and chisel, rebate plane or router (see the diagram opposite). Check the fit of each rebate. If routing, clamp all rails together with their ends flush, face side up (place scrap material on each side). Set the router to cut 6 mm deep. Maintain the same width of cut, or set up a fence and run the rebates on all rails at the same time.

21 Use a marking gauge or mortise gauge, a pencil and a square to mark the dowel positions (see the diagram opposite). Working from the inside face of each stile, use the gauge set to 7 mm to mark a 60 mm long line down from the top. Repeat this process for the bottom of each stile, marking 60 mm up. Reset the gauge and then mark 20 mm in from both ends of each rail, then 20 mm and

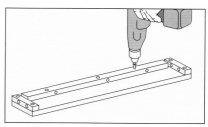

16 Glue the cleats in place and secure with evenly spaced screws. Stagger the screws.

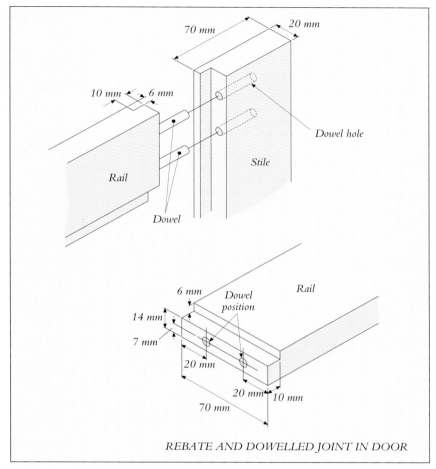

70 mm

20 mm

10 mm   6 mm

Dowel hole

Stile

Rail

Dowel

6 mm

Dowel position

Rail

14 mm

7 mm

20 mm

20 mm   10 mm

70 mm

REBATE AND DOWELLED JOINT IN DOOR

50 mm from the top and bottom of the stiles.

22 Using a dowelling jig with a 6 mm bush and a power drill and twist bit, bore 26 mm deep holes on all centre lines.

23 Put adhesive in the dowel holes and spread some across the joint. Use

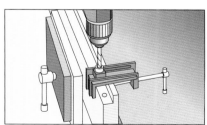

22 Using a dowelling jig and a drill and twist bit, bore 26 mm deep holes on all centre lines.

a pencil to apply adhesive and to remove any excess. Insert dowels in the holes in the rails and gently tap them in with a hammer. Push the pieces together. Clamp the stiles and rails together with sash cramps, ensuring they are square. Clean off excess adhesive. Leave to dry.

ASSEMBLING THE DOORS

24 When dry, remove the cramps. Plane the joints level if necessary. Check the fit of each door, then sand with 180 grit abrasive paper and finish with 220 grit.

25 Check the size of the rebated area and set the pre-cut glass panels into the rebate at the back of each door.

26 Protect the glass with cardboard and attach beads to the inside back edges of stiles and rails using panel pins (start with vertical beads). Punch the heads beneath the surface.

INSTALLING THE DOORS

27 Use concealed hinges to fit the door to the bookcase. Place the unit on its side with the hinging side

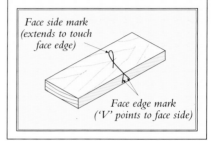

MARKING TIMBER

After planing and checking for straightness, mark the face side and edge of timber pieces in pencil. These marks help you quickly identify pieces, and indicate that two adjacent pieces are square to each other. Always work from the face side and edge.

Face side mark (extends to touch face edge)

Face edge mark ('V' points to face side)

down, and mark a centre line from the mounting plate position to the edge. Follow the manufacturer's instructions for fitting the hinges. Ensure that the hinge arm is at right angles to the door edge, and attach the door. Adjust as necessary.

28 Attach handles and apply the finish of your choice.

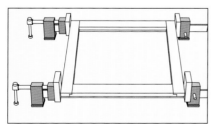

23 Clamp the stiles and rails together with sash cramps, ensuring that they are square.

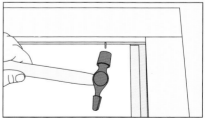

26 Protecting the glass with cardboard, attach the beads to the stiles and rails with panel pins.

Tools for building bookcases

Some of the most useful tools for making bookcases are shown below. Build up your tool kit gradually — most of the tools can be purchased from your local hardware store.

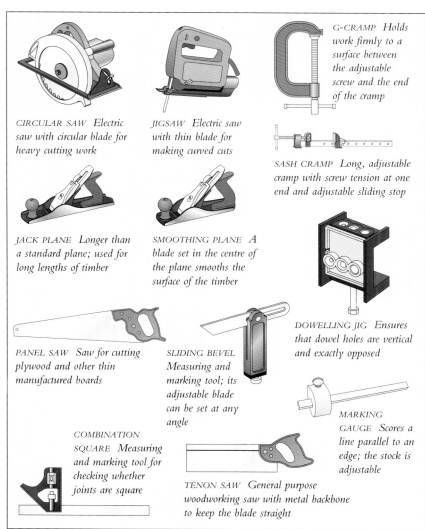

CIRCULAR SAW *Electric saw with circular blade for heavy cutting work*

JIGSAW *Electric saw with thin blade for making curved cuts*

G-CRAMP *Holds work firmly to a surface between the adjustable screw and the end of the cramp*

SASH CRAMP *Long, adjustable cramp with screw tension at one end and adjustable sliding stop*

JACK PLANE *Longer than a standard plane; used for long lengths of timber*

SMOOTHING PLANE *A blade set in the centre of the plane smooths the surface of the timber*

PANEL SAW *Saw for cutting plywood and other thin manufactured boards*

SLIDING BEVEL *Measuring and marking tool; its adjustable blade can be set at any angle*

DOWELLING JIG *Ensures that dowel holes are vertical and exactly opposed*

MARKING GAUGE *Scores a line parallel to an edge; the stock is adjustable*

COMBINATION SQUARE *Measuring and marking tool for checking whether joints are square*

TENON SAW *General purpose woodworking saw with metal backbone to keep the blade straight*

Index

TIMBER CONDITIONS

Timber is sold in three conditions:
- sawn or rough-sawn: sawn to a specific (nominal) size
- planed all round (PAR)
- moulded: shaped to a specific profile for architraves, skirting boards and so on.

Planed timber is mostly sold using the same nominal dimensions as sawn timber, for example 100 x 50 mm, but the surfaces have all been machined to a flat, even width and thickness so the '100 x 50 mm' timber is actually 91 x 41 mm. The chart shows the actual sizes for seasoned timber; unseasoned timber, such as radiata or hoop pine, will vary in size.

Moulded timbers are also ordered by nominal sizes, but check them carefully as there will be variations.

Sawn (nominal) size (mm)	Size after planing (mm)
19	15
25	19
38	30
50	41
75	66
100	91
125	115
150	138